Burnt

PJ Bayliss

Other titles by PJ Bayliss

Check out my author page on Amazon

Smutty Romance:

Librium
Risqué Liaisons: The Hot Lap

Poetry:

Restraint
Absence
Hush
How Deep Is Your Dog?

First published 2014
Re-released 2025

1 2 **3** 4 5 6 7 8 9

Cover photographs provided under copywriter license from
www.shutterstock.com

ISBN: 978-0-473-26891-6

DEDICATION

To the countless many who fell for an eternity as I took up the pen.

May the dogs be caged and your torn clothes repaired.

DEDICATION 2025

To the narcissistic apple seed that fell from the great tree.

May you slowly fester and rot where you lie until hell is ready to receive you.

2025 Memorandum

Ten years have passed since I first released this book...

I recall that my attitude and demeanor was about as dark as anyone could wish upon themselves. With every passing day, I put on the show of being a turbulent poet – so full of emotion it could have been considered sacrificial to society norms. I was aching to be discovered and all too eager to reveal a risqué inner self that was prepared to do anything to make my marque on the world.

We never discussed our feelings openly in my conservative corner of the world. Depression, anxiety, and neurodiversity concepts were still emerging among niche groups. Core values from previous generations of stiff-upper-lip white collar workers typically safeguarded these "mental diseases" from ever revealing themselves.

I remember pausing for months before finally publishing this book. My fear was of unfounded criticism and a sense of pending failure. Rejection maybe?

Ten years on and surprisingly not that much has changed.

The world population is still a captive audience watching cultures at war with each other.

The ugly beauty of the human spirit continues to invent new ways to explore social boundaries with confronting sexuality themes.

And I continue to pause briefly with the shadow of past rejection surrounding me once again, poised to swallow my soul up into the darkest obscurity poised and waiting ahead of me.

ACKNOWLEDGMENT

My deepest gratitude and thanks go out to all those who have encouraged and praised my writing and poetry in recent years. I have been truly humbled and deeply inspired by the comments you have provided over this time. I consider every single comment and note of support to be a valuable gift and without them I would never have considered putting this compilation together or pursuing my passion in writing.

Thanks to everybody who has guided me through this journey, especially the authors that I adore, friends who have mentored, and professionals in the writing industry who have advised me in my approach and delivery. You have always been so gracious with your time and honesty in your opinions, which are two of the highest commodities I could possibly ask for.

My sincerest appreciation goes to everyone who has joined me Online in Facebook, Twitter, and everywhere else. You have triggered a life-changing event within my life that I could not possibly anticipate in my wildest dreams. You are all so generous with your support and are such beautifully amazing people.

Finally, I thank you, the reader of this book, for taking the time out to embrace my work. It is only for you that I put these pages together and sincerely hope you enjoy this book.

2025 Addendum

To my special work colleague who has gently reminded me of my truth worth and value in life. These past few months have been nothing less than magical and the most memorable ever for all the learnings you provided.

FOREWORD

I had just finished playing with my son one evening and was reading a book to him when the latest world news started on television. He sat there quietly in my arms, suckling two fingers for comfort, as images of senseless violence from around the world flashed across the room.

These reports about the Houla massacre in Syria in mid-2012 affected me profoundly because I felt powerless to aid the victims. From my safe vantage point thousands of miles away, I watched in horror at the pained faces of parents and relatives who were coming to terms with the catastrophe. For many victims, there were no family members left to grieve for them.

My boy had barely started school a few weeks prior hand, so I certainly did not expect him to understand, yet alone question the images on the screen. First, he asked if the kids were just sleeping. Then he wanted to know what happened to the dead kids in their playground. Finally, he asked me why their daddies could not protect them from the bad guys, and he wanted my assurance that I would stop that from happening to him.

I couldn't answer him honestly and struggled to explain the situation.

And now, thanks to portable device technology, these gory pictures are regularly available and in the hands of my, and your own children around the world. My fatherly instincts kicked in as I ventured further into online social media communities and became horrified by what I saw.

At first, I simply observed and noticed the plethora of online communities, forums, applications, and web sites that exposed my family. The age restriction barriers were pointless because the most prolific social media company in the world supported the worst offending material.

It wasn't very long before the topic of violence evolved into a more sinister sexual nature with groups and pages that lured the youngest and most innocent into their realm.

What happened next is difficult to understand, let alone explain, but my darkest anxieties and deepest frustrations eventually took over my mind.

I grabbed a pen and began writing my thoughts, feelings, concerns, and questions into my diary. Some of these entries are completely illegible as my raw emotions spilled out onto the page. Minutes of angry frustration turned into months of hazy anxiety attacks where my only, sensible, control mechanism was writing.

Naturally, my coping mechanisms included drugs and alcohol as well, but poetry made one of the greatest differences to my life. In most occasions, my muse was a news headline, a scene within a novel, or situation I heard about through media. On other occasions, the verses evolved through sleep-depraved nightmares of terror and tragedy.

I continue to grieve daily, and I lay awake at night as the side effects of my prescriptions subside. There is barely a moment where I wish this journey could have been different, but then I realize that it is only just the beginning.

"He killed them with their love"

Stephen King
The Green Mile

NOCTURNAL TRAGEDY

For as long as I remember,
I have struggled to sleep,
Vacant in my slumber,
But forever dreaming.

Days became long,
Nights were too short,
Patience now destroyed,
My mind became taut.

Sheltering my eyes,
With both of my hands,
Searching for answers,
Lost emotions ran.

Like ink they fell,
Tears onto the paper,
Capturing each thought,
Of my own caper.

Unwilling to speak,
Verse became my voice,
I am completely lost,
Without any choice.

Flick through the leaves,
Reflecting my past,
Be rest assured,
It was quite a blast.

FRIEND

The sweeper was there in the club that day,
But I was too busy and could not stay,
He donated his time and gave us a smile,
Until he dropped one day while jogging a mile.

The red-nosed gentleman always said "Hi",
Eager to hear how my day had gone by,
Regardless of what went on in his life,
I heard of his death by his gracious wife.

We drove down the road and bumped into the guy,
Who had suddenly stopped in order to die,
Despite nearby doctors going hard to work,
Just goes to show, death always lurks.

My Grandfather always seemed grumpy and mean,
Until one afternoon he coughed up his spleen,
He was strong willed and always merry with beer,
My last words to him had made my feelings quite clear.

The dust barely settles as he falls on foreign soil,
A journalist captures the moment blood spoils,
The uniformed father with his kids playing at home,
Who learn of his death when online they roam.

I sit in my bunker and peer through my eyes,
Hiding from this world and my untimely demise,
Calmly putting everything to the test,
Running from the night where I never rest.

My existence resides in a corridor of time,
Caring for lives who are not mine,
Rolling messages and pages of words,
Content with my ending, if I am never heard.

TIME TO TIME

Time just keeps ticking along,
Like the lyrics in a love song,
In a past world without any wrong,
Just constant fear of falling bombs.

Landing within crowded streets,
Where sweaty cops brave the beat,
It is never the enemy we see,
For they look just like you and me.

They shoot from the wings,
Like puppets on strings,
Not human beings,
As the chorus sings.

Soldiers fall within the crowd,
Beneath a looming mushroom cloud,
They fought hard and so proud,
Against hidden fearless cowards.

What can I possibly say,
To my loving kids each grueling day,
"Justice shall come" as they say,
But we sit tight and quietly pray.

With dry eyes, I continue crying,
For this world of war crime,
As screams of children's death rhyme,
Forever and ever throughout time.

STOP

Every morning when I rise,
I submit myself to mechanical tide,
Noxious fumes sweeping spirits away,
As the dawn breaks in a brand new day.

Dusty tears soak through my cold hide,
Glazed expressions mirror me each side,
Reflections of despair constantly display,
From within ironed pressed suits of grey.

News headlines torment me every night,
Sad tales of torture while freedom fights,
I'm living under a tiny glimmer of hope,
Where petty cash buys your own rope.

It is barely a life amidst the masses,
Breathing in our own toxic gasses,
Gorging upon fruit from the tree,
While watching global poverty.

Lust,
Romance,
To love one another,
Yet kill someone's brother.

When will it ever be enough?
Stop   the   pain.

PJ BAYLISS

MY AFFLICTION

Empty voices echo on city streets,
Against full buildings built with concrete,
At least that's what they're supposed to do,
As traffic stirs thick like a meat stew.

I hear the cries from where we can't see,
Amidst acres of forests filled with trees,
Felled for gossip pages and timber,
To inform and bury the modern sinner.

Distant echoes from distant land,
By falling children as blood stains the sand,
Parents assuring them nothing is wrong,
Beneath the shadow of the falling bomb.

I can't help but think this is completely wrong,
Silence deafens me as their voices are gone,
I used to think that our dreams were free,
You have no idea what's brewing in me.

I cannot simply lie down and rest,
As I fear I shall fall to my death,
Every night I relive their screams,
Let the mists of time scrub my memory.

It's just one chapter in my life,
One I prefer not to read but to write,
Just one grain of sand in this passage of time,
So don't treat me as if I've lost my mind.

If I was ever here, it's because I was gone,
Lost in this crowd living right and wrong,
Pretentious smiles are all I see anymore,
Let me tear open 'til my heart hits the floor.

It's not as if that would be noticed,
Who'd even notice if I slid into the bliss,
If my time came up upon this busy street,
It would simply become yet another beat.

With my name etched in a cold slab of grey,
Nobody mourning for my soul to stay,
It pains me to think that could be it,
My carcass rotting in a damp pit.

A cold salty tear crawls down my cheek,
To become the make-up of a bottled freak,
Yet you wonder why I curl up and cry,
As streams of tears fall from the sky.

My humane affliction always appears,
To confront life itself without any fear,
Spilling ink like blood as I now write,
While the mortality counter predicts my plight.

It's the only way I can avoid that gate,
To take control of my own fervent fate,
I cannot stop the pouring sands of time,
At least I can stop to write my own line.

LOST EARTH

At first we were creatures,
Now here we all are,
In this celestial lab,
Within a glass jar.

Pleading our innocence,
Underneath the scope,
Perched on our doorsteps.
Searching for hope.

Beneath the heavens,
Under the sheets,
Just a boy and a girl,
Two insignificant beasts.

Within this pre-loved world,
There's no-one else to blame,
As we destroy life each day,
Without any shame.

Carved by biblical floods,
Soil torn into slithers,
We turn water into sewage,
To pollute our rivers.

The fattening corporations,
Accept no hidden flaws,
They purchase stretch limos,
To fund on-going wars.

Why don't we ever stop?
Those production lines,
That cause corpses to rot,
Around billets of lead?

Upon cut rainforest trees,
We write slogans on paper,
Let us do what we please,
Save our world for later.

We hold firm our phones,
In case we capture that shot,
Of a jumbo jet falling,
Or that child time forgot.

So, if everything fails,
What does it matter?
Memory cards will prevail,
Should the earth shatter.

I guess we'll become,
An archaeological find,
Funded by aliens,
At some distant time.

As our beacon of hope,
Continues through space,
Please return to lost earth,
We destroyed it through faith.

PJ BAYLISS

ABUNDANCE OF ONSLAUGHT

From across the field,
Peaceful and green,
Comes the sound,
Of crickets' unseen.

Gathering of small footprints,
Amidst the white sand,
Scattered toys and trikes,
Decorate the land.

The sun settling in,
For the dark night,
Paints the field red,
A beautiful sight.

In my small little world,
Everything seems right,
Amidst hugs and kisses,
Barely anyone fights.

Regrettably though,
This view is not shared,
For in a world far away,
Souls bathe in tears.

An abundance of onslaught,
Could possibly describe,
This land far away,
Where the innocent die.

From across the desert,
Desolate and hot,
Comes the sound,
Of many gunshots.

The guns rattle on,
Into the night,
Tracers marking the kill,
A miserable sight.

Clusters of bombs,
Fall from the sky,
Scattering limbs,
Everyone dies.

I cannot imagine,
What their life must be like,
Where death constantly lurks,
Throughout day and night.

As I kiss my own child,
Upon their forehead,
Their smiles are common,
As are fields painted red.

A silence falls around me,
Deafness ringing in my ears,
I'm awake yet still dreaming,
Battling my own fears.

CLAYTON'S MASSACRE

Can you spare just one thought?
Without finding blame,
For whom were slaughtered,
Or left hobbling in pain.

For their freedom they fight,
From behind cast iron gates,
Each day into the night,
Passion derives their own fate.

For they began the day,
Waking with their fears,
Rubbing shoulders to pray,
Before spilling tears.

Their brethren falling,
Crumbling into dust,
Lead bullets soaring,
Into souls' they thrust.

We watch as their shadows,
Slowly fill with spilt blood,
From the comfort of home,
When will enough be enough?

This torturous massacre,
Continues day after day,
In the land where heat seekers,
Are guided toward their prey.

TWIST OF FATE

Why am I tortured through the night?
Why should this be a brutal test?
Leaving me without any fight,
Tossing and turning as I rest.

Shrill echo of dawn awakens me,
Before the sun reveals the day,
Removed from slumbers ecstasy,
Enslaved to work to remain free.

A cup of Joe quickly poured,
Freshly pressed iron suit I adorn,
I depart from those whom I adore,
As the rising sun barely warms.

My soul outlined by black suit,
Motionless yet travelling,
Grouped like rats led by a flute,
Mindless thoughts unreeling.

To the mill I grind, labor and work,
Assigning names to numbers,
My mind for rent without perks,
'Till night brings me cruel slumber.

Cruel twist of fate bludgeons me,
As work was once my passion,
Now it taunts the soul within me,
With torment you could not imagine.

PJ BAYLISS

YOU THINK

You think you are the best,
You think you are so right,
You think I am a mess,
You think I'm such a sight.

I'm here to tell you,
This thing you have must stop,
This thing you oppress me with,
Will eventually send me to rot.

I'm not going to shout,
Or beg upon bended knee,
You missed this last opportunity,
Now just stop impeding me.

You think I know so much less,
Than you give me credit for,
You think my ears are deaf,
And I won't walk out that door.

That door I once walked through,
And you were there with her,
Shouting as if I was wrong,
You complete and total wanker.

I'm no longer there,
To lay your sad woes upon,
I'm never going to regret,
Choosing the chosen one.

Why should I stop and listen,
To your freakish nightmares,
When you shunned me,
As I faced my greatest fears.

You watched me break down,
With my shattered heart,
Thinking I was the clown,
Quietly falling apart.

You think I'm coming home,
Where my soul died inside,
Back to your loveless zone,
Where you choose to hide.

You think I'm kidding,
This time it is for real,
I'm happy now you've gone,
Happy to finally heal.

And don't you ever think,
I'd ever have any regrets,
Or your shit doesn't stick,
Farewell, you flamin' pest.

You think too much.

SEA OF PAIN

Primeval slurry of desolate names,
The hungry, scarred, barren, and enslaved,
I wade into the abyss beyond depth of my knee,
To be flogged, chastised, beckoned to heed.

Amongst friendly chatter a dark evil lurked,
Identifying victims and how the red room worked,
Master's voice boomed like a heavy bass drum,
Naked bodies writhing with fluid emotion.

From shoreline I realized what had to be done,
And pitied the fragility of this kingdom,
In guise I approached as Eve not as Adam,
To be hustled, and accosted by angels of Satan.

I was but titan under cover of the still night,
Spellbound maidens merely sought lusts delight,
Foul Master objected to my verse that lingered,
He eradicated all men with one tap from his finger.

The protector was vanquished, hung out to dry,
A poor child stood brave with tears in her eye,
To the sea of pain I returned once again,
Salvaging souls before they were abandoned.

A revelation of love and praise from the roses,
Lifting thy sword to swing down with prose,
Now the toxic sea recedes to its end,
I emerged, triumphant, with friends.

THE JOURNEY

Down incline I stride,
I am so terrified inside,
The toxic fog resides,
Inside thy skull's hide.

At rock bottom. Snap,
A violent crack,
White flesh turns black,
Red topples from stack.

A whisper and crook,
Fluttering leaves of books,
Pitch soul, seeping brook,
Somber, petrified look.

Lost luminescence,
My immortal essence,
Hacked open crescent,
Interred thy peasant.

Strained gasmask hides,
My deep burning inside,
Passionate desire,
Pitch cast on pyre.

Red ooze is freed,
Amidst fog I breathe,
Revelation, can it be,
My discovered entity.

Wading from surf,
Through red afterbirth,
Soaked to my girth,
I scour this earth.

I choose not to reveal,
I will not cut peal,
Pitch can't up keel,
I must begin heal.

I pause and grin,
I breathe from within,
A shiver ignites sin,
Static crawls across skin.

I relax face,
Providing them space,
We heal within grace,
Within our small place.

Release I could,
Trust I surely would,
Our love is so good,
As they knew it would.

Welded as friends,
Pitch journey ends,
Tight gas-mask blends,
Writing entity mends.

MASK

As my feet hit the ground,
Moment in place,
Alarm clocks buzzing,
In distant space.

I step into watery heat,
Ambrosia surrounds me,
My soul reels in retreat,
She overwhelms me.

Slumber washes down the drain,
With memories of the past,
A slow release of my pain,
Peeling off my tight mask.

Merging ribbons of grey,
Forbidden lust within me,
For I begin every day,
Wishing my lover completes me.

I seek desperately,
My passion, love, pride,
Seeking council from thee,
Though in shadow, you hide.

My words echo from the night,
I please should you ask,
Unraveling my lover's plight,
From beneath my black mask.

3-RED, 1-BLUE

Red for my head,	Blue for my bed,
3-Red,	1-blue,
Red is Sad,	Bad to Eat,
Changes Face,	Spoils my Taste,
Places a nice smile,	Removes sting in tail,
Takes away that dam hum,	Takes me out within round one,
Must be taken with food,	Removes dreams that are rude,
Can make you twitch,	Makes eating a bitch,
Removes the hue,	Splits me into two,
Provides a thrill,	Too many will kill,
Makes my day,	Takes night away,
3-Red,	1-blue,
Boo,	Hoo.

SAVE ME

Did an absence of love dig this hole in my mind?
Did I have any other choice other than to stumble?
Into the dark wilderness to rescue the blind,
Or was it simply another aspect of life?

Was it even a choice?
Or was it something else?
Compassion?
Fear?
Sensuality?

Do you really think,
I'm trying to avoid any help?
Are you kidding?
Am I clinically mad?
Why don't you,
Save me?

There simply is no more space left inside my head,
Only logical squares,
Ticks,
And boxes instead.

My insides are twisted,
Distorted,
Full of despair,
My beating heart is in need of repair.

Passion,
Romance,
Music,
My urge for art.
All of the above,
It's tearing me apart.

Pulling me to pieces,
Ripping away at my soul,
Filling me with grief,
Filling up my dark hole.

Is that what you want my life to be?
Full of life,
A "life" that appears free.

But it's not,
Not for you,
Not for me.

Save me.

I have days that come and go,
All the time,
To and fro.

These days are just grey,
Dusty and blurred,
Shadows,
Twisted,
Just simply disturbed.

I whisper with a scream.

SAVE ME.

Why must I continue to live that way?
My insides bottled up,
Compacted,
Stored away.

Why must I learn how not to shout?
My soul buried,
Not allowed to get out.

Why must I live like that until I die?
Among the crowd,
Tailored suits,
With colleagues,
Not companions,
And a fist full of dollars,
With a wallet full of debt.

SAVE ME!

Save me from this fucking mess,
Save me from that world of glass,
Save me from being myself,
Save me from my personal hell,
Save me from the world of fear,
Save me...
...just stay near.

UNTITLED #NO. 3

What is the fucken point,
For carrying this on?
I never get it right,
Always getting it wrong.

If it's not enough money,
I've haven't spent enough,
Maybe I'm too gentle,
Or else I'm too rough.

Yet when I explained my need,
A dream to win a goal,
I was merely laughed at,
Humbly ridiculed.

It's such a fine edge,
Like that of a blade,
Shimmering so bright,
Beckoning me to play.

It's so bloody simple,
With the answer right there,
Washing down my sorrow,
Until I no longer care.

I doubt I shall be missed,
By any but just a few,
Who never dried my tears,
If only they knew.

EXIST

I'm waiting for one of 'those calls'
That involves a dear friend,
May not have seen him since last fall,
But 'E-N-D' still spells end.

He is in good hands,
Or so they all say,
Tagged name in a band,
In case it's needed the next day.

Near departed souls of land,
Maybe someone else's mate,
Who may need a new patch,
Prior to knock on the gate.

Or possibly sent toward the pitch?

So time stays dead still,
Words echo through my room,
Shaking from lack of pill,
Least there is no more rat boom.

We fill our soul while we sit,
Wash our salts and quench,
Food never fills this deep pit,
We are all players in the shit.

A bell signals' message of news,
To earth our personal fears,
A few words would induce spew,
Others would bring cheers.

The mighty power of words,
Delivers more than deep shock,
Nervously, I write some blurbs,
My emotions kept in stock.

It is still a beautiful day,
Blue skies and clouds in sky,
It is what some people may say,
A fantastic day to die.

If there is ever such time,
Place or ideal situation,
Life's passage of rhyme,
Sends tingles of sensation.

Last night when she called,
There was panic in her voice,
Obviously, she had balled,
As if there was one choice.

Hey, that's what they do,
The white coats and nurses,
"Here is the honest truth,
As you fill our purses".

That's our worse fear,
But I have done what I can,
For my friend torn in pieces,
He always knew who I am.

A man of few words,
I just sit still on this hill,
I know death will persist,
I write when my mind is still,
I bleed daily to exist.

BALLAD OF BLUES

The humble host was locked away,
Your world barren and void,
Salty sea breeze blowing your way,
Where land was once destroyed.

A young boy you once used to be,
Your innocent youth was slain,
Lost in a search for destiny,
Found in a pool of pain.

Searching for answers in distant stars,
When love belonged within,
Your soul recently ripped apart,
Body immersed in sin.

The devil of fate held your hand,
As the angel sheltered,
Led away to a promised land,
Where fortune was honored.

Pack your easel and brush away,
Leave your conscience behind,
Embrace big city lights today,
Leave that warm sun behind.

Adorn this tailored cotton suit,
And remember to punch in,
Dance in tune to the devil's flute,
Your soul shall embrace sin.

Just a pawn in the numbers game,
In a boat you shall not rock,
Forced to appease them with filthy shame,
Right down to your tailored socks.

Join the procession with the others,
Quaffing java in the daily grind,
Till the smog of progress does smother,
Gassing you out of your mind.

Do your duty and nothing else,
Prepare to receive more abuse,
Cower at night in your warm house,
With your necktie as a noose.

You really are so pathetic,
Hidden so deep inside,
Expecting wealth like it's magic,
Crippling your weary hide.

Time has run out for you my friend,
You knew this deep within,
Living life as if it must end,
Gifting your spirit to sin.

HOLDING IT TOGETHER

I can't explain,
This feeling inside,
Feeling so lost,
Yet longing to hide.

It taunts me each day,
Tears me in half,
Squeezing me in,
Pulling me apart.

I embrace the depth,
Immersed in its wash,
Where I find myself,
Forever I'm lost.

With my every breath,
I watch my life pass,
Inhaling its scent,
As if it's my last.

But I still see your smirk,
Through my blurred tears,
Looking at me that way,
Like I'm your worst fear.

Raising your eyes,
As my hand quivers,
Blind to my pain,
While I die and wither.

I struggle not to release,
The silver blade of justice,
To let my congealing juice leak,
Over my tightly closed fist.

Waiting for an eternity,
As you rush to my side,
Trying to hold it together,
Deep seams in my hide.

My soul hemorrhaging,
Spilling over the floor,
Lost forever now,
I am no more.

Do you really care,
If I am so lost?
I'm here, after all,
To punch in the clock.

Why should I try,
To explain my own mess,
When it's so obvious,
You believe you are blessed.

Just leave me right here,
Alone in the dark,
While I reach for my dreams,
To leave my own mark.

WE CAN'T DEFINE

This black hole inside me,
Just keeps on growing,
It's so dam frightening,
I simply ... can't define.

I'm no longer residing,
Inside I'm declining,
Without understanding,
Who, what, ...where and why.

I'm lost so completely,
Yet waiting discretely,
Until it defeats me,
I breakdown and cry.

This feeling subdues me,
My burnt soul is left bleeding,
From pain I'm still conceiving,
I quite simply cannot define.

Why would you leave me this way?
Whatever made you think you could play,
With my fragile heart in that way?
You've filled my entire life with dismay.

You are on my mind every day,
I cannot forget come what may,
You're the only pain I want to stay,
No matter how I cringe from your flay.

You once thought you could free me,
Or maybe complete me,
Through torturous seething,
Until ... I decide.

Despite the shoving and heaving,
All the ecstatic breathing,
You knew I would not flee,
No matter how you tried.

You cut me up so intensely,
But I could never bleed,
As my heart no longer beats,
From the very day you lied.

Now my soul shall repair me,
Through scars as my destiny,
Shall become my epiphany,
Through love you can't define.

INNOCENT CHILD

Why do they cry?
He asked me tonight,
As we watched parents scream,
Upon that television screen.

I could only sigh,
Thinking of how I could lie,
To my innocent son,
Who uses a finger as a gun.

We watched in vain,
As blood curdling pain,
Echoed across the street,
From parents at their bare feet.

It's a war I said,
So now the ground is red,
But it's best if you don't know,
Let's grab a ball and play throw.

We played together outside,
The dog panting at our side,
It was a magical delight,
Just my son, the dog, and I.

We played until dusk,
Just the dog and us,
Before innocent voice said,
Daddy, why does the sky turn red?

Why do you ask my son?
So curious and young,
And then he said to me,
I was just thinking.

If it was the war you said,
Turning the sky over there red,
Then maybe I could help?
He said with a gentle pout.

A single tear broke free,
To trickle down my cheek,
As I then hugged my son,
Who wiped it away with his gun.

No matter how I lie,
Or explain that red sky,
There is nothing it seems,
That will reduce the screams.

Will you cuddle them tonight,
As tears cloud up the sky,
From the innocent child,
So desperate and wild.

4.09.43

Beyond the gentle drops of rain,
That crawl softly down my face,
Mingle tears of my heartfelt pain,
Drawn from this putrid, human race.

Their clothes were soaked in warm blood,
Spilt by rebels behind the wall,
Bystanders wading into the flood,
To retrieve lost souls as they fall.

I close my eyes and cast a tear,
Over Mother Nature's glossy stain,
I'm forced to look away in despair,
For I can't help all those who are slain.

We like to grieve for those who care,
Their memories provide us life,
Our real emotions we try to bare,
Our feelings we prefer to hide.

Families hiding behind locked doors,
With windows shut each night,
While victims crawl across the floor,
Lurking in shadows beyond our sight.

I watch this faux pas of society,
Without conviction to be found,
With motives beyond you or me,
Trailing the stench of hell's hound.

Let's face it, without hell below,
There's no point in heaven above,
We may not adorn a bright halo,
Yet we still fight for white peace doves.

Would peace ensure safety from harm?
I'm just so curious to know,
My only peace is with your arms,
When you hold me so tight I cannot go.

Although we lock ourselves away,
Or even try to lock the evil up,
The hounds still come night and day,
As passion delivers new pups.

What is passion? I'm forced to say,
As it resides in everyone's eyes,
Including those who plot all day,
To ensure somebody dies.

Passion is shared by friend and foe,
And those who fight for common cause,
So many forms I do not know,
Always present as death within wars.

The rain now falls upon this earth,
From grey clouds high above,
With my tears they soak the turf,
In this world soaked through with love.

UNTITLED #NO. 4

Have you ever,
Thought that dammit,
We have destroyed,
Our own planet?

Have you ever,
Wondered why,
We're taught to love,
Yet trained to die?

Have you ever,
Worked a day,
With extra hours,
Without the pay?

Have you ever,
Seen their eyes?
The lost youth,
Are they blind?

Have you ever,
Ignored the views,
Of the victims,
Upon the news?

Have you ever,
Heard their words,
Across the ocean,
As they burn?

Have you ever,
Asked yourself?
Is this heaven?
Or is it hell?

I have never,
Felt this fate,
Nor accepted,
It's too late.

PJ BAYLISS

JUST ONE DAY

Don't you realize what I've become,
Or that my heart's no longer one,
Through tears of pain it's split in two,
Neither half is there for you,
I remain lost and still undone.

It feels like everyone is blind,
But still I chase my own lost time,
Forgetting childhood memories,
Lungs so tight, I dare not breathe,
I feel so at home in the sublime.

The news broadcast displays the dead,
Kids who never woke from their own bed,
Parents crying and laying blame,
Have we lost our sense of shame,
Or just avoiding our own dread.

Working each moment to buy the next,
Communicating via cell phone text,
Daydreaming through each day,
Awake each night with dismay,
None of it makes any sense.

And yet we rarely ever question why,
One man lives as another dies,
Bodies strewn across the sand,
Blood stains on the still hand,
Against the setting skies.

WADE

I no longer feel right with you,
Always doubting my point of view,
Never knowing right from wrong,
Should I listen or sing my song.

It's impossible to feel comfortable,
Am I your hero or just a fool,
Am I now a stranger under the cover?
Once guiding light now lost lover.

I no longer know how to act,
Strange it seems but it's a fact,
Impossible to know what you need,
A moment of silence or symphony.

Everyone say I've lost the plot,
So much so that it does not,
Feel the same when we kiss,
Upon your lips or within your bliss.

There's a gentle part of me within,
That feels estranged when I grin,
I appear so strong, but I still fade,
Into a sea of despair where I wade.

BIRDSONG

The desolate rain fades away,
To rinse dilated black glare,
Illuminated within the night,
I sensed her,
Standing there.

I envision,
Imagine,
My numb mind gathers more.

My fantasy,
Divinity,
Shackled,
Sensual receipt in the raw.

As softly she spoke,
Barely noticing me there,
From sweet dream I woke,
"Comply me my Dear"

I resign myself.

Leniently we touch,
Connecting then we merge,
My fingers running,
Softly,
Across her refined verge.

With strengthening blood,
I reduce my space,
Grasping,
Commanding,
To hasten our pace.

Slowly I withdraw,
Caressing shoulder and neck,
Now filled with lust,
Firmly hauling her right back.

We writhe,
Intertwine,
Locking ourselves in,
Drawing the exotic nectar,
From her delicate sin.

The ponderous rain ceases to pour outside,
Winds collapsing,
To a silent sigh.

I embrace her flaming shoulder,
As my soul pours her desert dry,
She grasps for restitution,
Emitting a small hollow cry.

Across distant cold breeze,
Birdsong echoes from the trees.
Singing together,
Gradually wilting,
Like fallen leaves.

She whispers my name,
I love you,

...Mon Ami.

SEARCHING

The still chill of autumn knocks upon my door,
As white petals quietly fall from the rose,
I no longer know who I am looking for,
My eyes now darken in light of prose.

Songbirds of lust haunt the shadows of dawn,
Frozen words drift upon the breeze,
To celebrate the day that I now loathe,
The child within me quietly flees.

I travel through seasons as if they rhyme,
As grey shards shiver across my back,
Open fingers filtering the sands of time,
That slowly fall through the cracks.

With patience I wait biding my time,
In a world that adores punishing smacks,
Black ink slowly crawls across the page,
Blood on our pavements dull with age.

I search high and low for what lies deep inside,
Avoiding the comfort of the reapers cloak,
Amidst day I still smile while at night I shall cry,
Always living in a haze of life's smoke.

Searching for a lost love I once had to hide,
Doomed to survive on this edge of hope,
Endlessly looking for something I need,
Not noticing the wound from where I bleed.

PJ BAYLISS

REBORN

Late one night under a moonlight glow,
I questioned my life and alter ego,
Am I the dunderhead that had it all wrong,
Was I just a chorus in someone else's song?

Reminiscing to the voice of an owl,
Wondering what life really means now,
Other than surviving my own death each night,
I am incapable of separating wrong from right.

Idling along the highway so grey,
I watched as the reaper took his life away,
Caught up in traffic without any flow,
The ambulance left with nowhere to go.

That day I'd worn a suit like a senator,
Living the dream to be a cash generator,
Climbing corporate walls to climb out of the gutter,
These elusive heights turning me into a nutter.

Foul stench of the land drifting upwind,
Falling from man and his infernal sin,
I continued to wipe the dried salt from my eye,
With memories fading of that time passing by.

With the crowd I abscond from the dream,
Into a reality that's virtually unseen,
Submitting myself to now live with the hoards,
I wrapped my torn wrists from where blood poured.

PROPHESY

I'm a writer,
Not shipwrecked,
My letters won't be jammed in a bottle,
Tossed to the sea.

You're a reader,
Not a beach,
Why risk the surf,
When you can swim within me.

I'm a lover,
Not a leader,
My emotions swirl over,
They consummate me.

You're a spirit,
Not a vice,
Compulsion to live,
Driving every need.

I'm a soul,
Not a being,
Never there,
Forever seen.

You're a beauty,
Not a disgrace,
Out of my sight,
Is out of place.

I'm abundant in treasure,
Always there waiting,
When you seek luxury.

You're a fruit from the gods,
The thirst from your harvest,
Fulfills my prophesy.

PJ BAYLISS

HEARTBREAK

I held you so closely in my arms,
Still you managed to evade my heart,
Struggling to save this world from harm,
Instead I was burnt alive and torn apart.

Delicate flesh cooking upon my bones,
Crispy tender and yet delicate moist,
Imprisoned within my own home,
Lost without any voice.

I sheltered deep amidst my fears,
Within toxic clouds of black anxiety,
Drowning within deep pools of tears,
Struggling against my sacrificial liberty.

Fighting daily against the reaper's urge,
To penetrate through my pale layer,
Where only the darkest evil lurks,
Unabated by the Lord's Prayer.

This putrid oil of my soul,
Slowly ebb and drift away,
Recessing back into a deep hole,
Where you know I shall obey.

Ushering back the tide of life,
Translucent like deep still water,
Washing away any remaining fight,
'Till my artist of desire is slaughtered.

There I shall remain forever,
Drifting hopelessly upon dead seas,
Surging against the stormy weather,
Being swept away from my destiny.

Till swirling currents of cruel fate,
Shipwreck me upon your beach,
A gentle snap of my heartbreak,
Within your arms yet out of reach.

PJ BAYLISS

AFTERCARE

There is an urge to explain various welts and pain,
As they were wrapped in darkness, pity, and vain,
Separated, I sit, and quietly reside beside myself,
Through black holes I peered, drained of inner health,
I cannot exist as one without living the other,
Poetic voices within propel an ice-cold shudder.

I told him.
He listened.

Red swirl in his brain broke over the levy,
Eyes wide open he could not see it was me,
So he bore down on my hide with great force,
My resilience was too weak, drained of course,
He passed over his liquid as if it was wine,
I admitted that this scene was my first time.

I questioned.
He answered.

The pair of us sat humbly in the sun,
With myself beside me, still joined as one,
Separated only by fragile panes of glass,
I eased into a comfortable pace at last,
The surrounding fog had begun to chill,
Tension released to welcome the thrill.

He commanded.
I complied.

The fog now removed from within my eyes,
I caught my own truth, to my own surprise,
I had not brutally torn myself apart,
It was just a mere fault of my aching heart,
He revealed his own love waiting quietly near,
How history split apart what they now share.

He scorned me.
I already knew.

PJ BAYLISS

FLOGGER OF DEATH

Strapping on tainted leather glove,
My mighty flogger is then charged,
Her deep lusty throaty growl,
Echoes across the land.

My flogger ripped through her white flesh,
Spilling a speck of pink,
Gnawing away with determined desire.

As I sliced down through her V,
She resisted abruptly,
I applied,
Flogger tried, patiently.

With undeniable force she gave,
And then breached,
My sanctuary held fast,
Head rushing, I almost passed.

With force constant applied,
Her advance was denied,
Head blood in retreat,
She lay,
Submitted at my feet.

PERFECT NIGHT

Amidst the dark night ahead,
My heart skips a beat,
And dreams turn wild,
For a stranger I met.

He dominates my lust,
And churns up a storm,
Capsizing inner goddess,
Overflowing with warmth.

His true intention is clear,
For love to embrace me,
Hence I listen all night,
To call his name.

Mon Ami.

SERENDIPITY

I walked out of classes,
Dyed my long hair,
Grew up with no hassles,
Barely a care.

My passion for art,
Poetic flair,
Raised without talent,
Or advised it was there.

Beaten and kicked,
Always pushed down,
My life as a kid,
Caused me to frown.

Tiny glimmers of hope,
Teachers who cared,
I worked for myself,
At the expense of peers.

For the price of a kiss,
I'd sell you my soul,
Inside I was content,
But I was never whole.

My life took a turn,
When I once drowned,
And climbed every ladder,
In this little town.

My ambition took hold,
I had no net worth,
Satisfied through lust,
Filling the moist purse.

Childhood disappeared,
My illusions were real,
Seeking a pure kiss,
Now I longed to heal.

From height I observed,
Corporate worlds below,
Pain from my past,
Now started to show.

Now I missed my peers,
How ironic was that,
I dived deep into mist,
Where my mind was black.

Not knowing where to go,
Nor able to turn back,
Submerged in love's abyss,
Seeping through my crack.

It was pure luck I guess,
Or maybe stupidity,
I just remember the mess,
Of my own serendipity.

TWISTED SPLICE

The toxic portal beacons as I sleep,
Homage to restless voices that I keep,
Blue drug induced cover slides away,
Revealing yet another fucking day.

The plane of light levitates above,
Gliding past like a silent dove,
Ticking of time pounding my head,
Blackened eyes streaked bloodied Red.

Playful demons pulsating under skin,
Spiritual nuance constrains passage in,
Residing passengers are very agitated,
His expressions erupt as now aggravated.

Tailored cloth embellish flesh color,
We survive dreary days after each other,
Should I not disturb the transit air,
My breath would forever linger there.

Sacrificial souls shuffle upon granite,
Tireless hours burnt to save dead planet,
Steel chambers humble the crowds,
Praise and reward to the plundering proud.

Whatever happened to the leading unique?
Those whom care or protect those who seek,
Success defined: a collection of embossed card,
With custom tailored cloth to hide rich lard.

Dare not perceive me as fallen from peak,
As I rise from my cast shadow as unique,
Nor is my imprudent mind a twisted grain,
Barren soul rinsed by foaming sea of pain.

The dawn, dusk, and space in between,
No longer offer any veracious meaning,
Now I find comfort with pumping rose,
To form stream of Black 'n' White prose.

PULLED APART

How do I start,
This is the end,
My mind's torn apart,
My questionable friend,
Continuing on with life,
Simply frightens me.

Some time ago,
Beyond reasoning,
I was a mere puppet,
Controlled by taut strings,
But they were broken in half,
Then I was stored in a case.

My limbs crumpled together,
Crushed in the cold dark,
Tourniquet used as a tether,
Gaged to prevent remark,
My eyes remained open,
Blind to any love.

There I remained,
My lifeless soul entombed,
But I persisted in vain,
My barren life continued,
Numb without any cause,
Stripped bare of my pride.

No longer could I continue,
The pain spilling out,
From my mind split in two,
Pulled apart by the crowd,
Why would I resist,
This start to my end?

PJ BAYLISS

LOVES RETURN

Fate has swept me upon this beach,
Tossed from the surf of lover's breach,
Wasting away with dull faded driftwood,
Soaked in my tears and misunderstood.

Sun beats mercilessly against my hide,
Shipwrecked high upon life's low tide,
Withering to grey and brittle form,
'Till my soul is no longer warm.

Life resumes through tears,
Wakened by nightmares,
Waiting here silently,
For love to return,
To me.

PULL YOURSELF TOGETHER

You asked for this,
You sniveling little bitch,
Get your arse out from that case,
Come into to my fatal pitch.

Let the darkness surround,
Wrapping you up tight,
Embrace my bloodhounds,
They taunt you every night.

I'm not here to be blamed,
For your own bloody demise,
Hang your head in shame,
In weight of my reprise.

How dare you complain,
For your complicated life,
While they shelter from planes,
Dropping bombs to their plight.

Watch their lifeless bodies,
Collapse in a bloodied clump,
Explosions fade in a volley,
Limbs landing with a thump.

Take note of the headlines,
See the man killed his wife,
A girl drowned in wine,
Another missile takes flight.

Open your eyes,
You fucking great moron,
You are naïve and blind,
Their fate was forgone.

Listen closely now,
As I unlatch your case,
With these few pills I vow,
To put a smile on your face.

You're not pulled apart,
Just badly put together,
With a compassionate heart,
To chase rainbows in bad weather.

Of course, you couldn't see,
Any of this shit coming,
It was always your destiny,
To become a lifeless dummy.

Don't you wince now little bitch,
I'll release you from that case,
As my blade finds the pitch,
Tears shall flow down your face.

I shall empty your lifeless husk,
Wading through your warm blood,
Coldness arriving in the dusk,
Reuniting us in love.

BLACK SKY DAY

I shudder when I wake,
To the sun that rises,
It's such a lovely day,
Outside.

But inside...
...It's full of surprises.

It's always bleak,
Miserable,
But no rain,
Just damp where I weep,
Through unseen pain.

"Unseen",
I sigh,
Ignored or forgotten,
Unnoticed more like,
Now it's all gone rotten.

Congratulations,
Upon the ultimate submission,
One that's never found,
Yet it's always hidden.

Encased in a fear,
Of what I may say,
Or what you will hear,
Every fucking day.

Yet you continue to scoff,
With your white lipped grin,
Flipping me off,
Into my own sin.

It's an endless pool,
As deep as the sky,
Where I swim like a fool,
Nobody knows why.

And nobody even cares,
I'm left unattended,
In my own pool of despair,
Watched by the pretentious.

Like I said before,
Congratulations,
I'm submitted as a bitch,
Treated like a whore.

The sun now rises high,
Burning rain clouds away,
Searing my inner thigh,
Welcoming the black sky day.

MASTER

What is a MASTER?
But a mere soul drafted upon string,
Like a wooden toy puppet,
Vacant of finger ring.

Hung,
His limbs and mind,
Tongue and heart,
Strung so tight,
Could they rip him apart?

Lines so taut,
Poised delicately between sublime souls.
Faith,
Belief that a subtle tug,
Would lead one to fold.

Inclination to snap,
Stretch or fall apart.
Potentially rupture his heart.

A MASTER cannot dictate or command one to submit,
From torn earth,
They must gift him the right,
The right to remit.

One must provide desire to tension his bow,
To thrive and love,
To and fro.

A MASTER must first give to earn trust,
Respecting space,
Never to feign,
In order for one to willingly submit.
To call out his name.

Her echoes must not drift or outcry false lust,
It must be,
A whisper of love.

PJ BAYLISS

SLAVE POET

Lips sealed upon command,
As he motions towards his mast,
Threaded hair though fingers,
While his golden prose starts to cast.

Words whispered in midnight air,
She casts off inner doubt and fear,
Morning my love,
Flog my aching sorrow bare.

Slowly she rolls upon firm bed,
Revealing herself to his deep mind,
Agonizing dreams leaving his head,
Striking upon his words so kind.

Linen sheets cast over chamber,
Her eyes shut,
Tremble,
Searching for release.
Seeking for true love,
As never before,
Reaching inside seeking inner peace.

Together they weave a golden embrace,
Rhythmically writing upon blank page,
Willing to oblige at his last pace,
While loving together through a lost age.

Cast to his spell they seek new height,
Her feet cast astride for morning relief,
Steadfast working waters of doubt,
Stroking the slave poet beyond belief.

His hand reaches forth to silky hair,
Surrendering she opens wide to glory,
Hot lava soaks lips,
Mouth and throat,
As she impulsively bursts into his story.

BURDEN

They say it is deep red,
Pumping rich blood to head,
Inane beating resounds inside,
Sharp pain flogging the mind.

Life's true essence exists,
Within black space akin to fist,
Rose petals cover my heart,
So easily ripped, torn apart.

Though dollar bills may fix the tear,
That blew apart when you were near,
Blood of my soul spilt for miles,
Coldly dripping from your smile.

Not interested in any repair,
Mere looks aggravate my fear,
Upon sight of my cheerful laughter,
They interrogate what I am after.

I only asked for one return,
To a question that now burn,
You silence my curious mind,
You make denial seem so kind.

Exhausted is your first excuse,
Now too late its just abuse,
Headache is yet another,
Illness becomes my early departure.

I could lay pitched here at night,
Waiting for your mighty flight,
Instead tears dampen my skin,
Rotting away my love within.

My salty ponds grow in doubt,
Tears ignite with flame from my pout,
Shattered heartbeat makes me tremble,
Emptying me of my former resemble.

I schedule life into me,
I see blood flow from me,
Leeched out from you no less,
Your innocence is my fucking mess.

What the bloody hell am I to do,
To turn back years not just these few,
You barely let me put a word in,
Packed tight I cram in more burden.

ONE

Left alone with your thoughts,
While your innocence leaks,
Neither captured nor caught,
Beneath the blindfold you peek.

Sensing my dark presence,
Resting within my shadow,
Bound tight in acceptance,
I approach you... from below.

You gasp with desire,
Upon the stubble from my chin,
Muzzling your inner thigh,
Caressing the lace upon your sin.

I tighten the velvet shackle,
Prying your ankles apart,
Muscular torso you straddle,
We writhe to your beating heart.

I touch my lip to yours,
Whispering your name,
Desire within now pours,
This urge... it's insane.

"Do you want me my dear?
How deep? and how long?
Will you release? Without fear?
Can't you see? We belong."

You are compelled to thrust,
Against my hardening girth,
Restrained tight in our trust,
I rest upon your wet purse.

With my finger I flick,
The elastic from your thigh,
I sense you are so slick,
Licking my fingers, you sigh.

I roll you,
Under my thumb,
I control you,
Until you are numb.

As my fingers crawl,
Hidden inside,
Massaging the walls,
Your nerves subside.

Lost, yet so aware,
You don't know how,
Demanding without a care,
"Fuck me... now."

I comply of course,
For it's you that I love,
Entering you as we forge,
Fitting together like a glove.

Edging me further in,
Deeper as you breathe,
Submersed in your sin,
Wearing you like a sleeve.

Now let our patience play,
As I embrace you from inside,
Our bodies rocking away,
While our souls glide.

Capture me within your eyes,
Gather me in your arms,
Locked between your thighs,
You surround me like a charm.

Woven together nice n' tight,
Your essence dripping onto me,
Nothing else feels so right,
You melt away with ecstasy.

Force yourself past that point,
When your body wants to stop,
With every thrust you soon anoint,
My firm and hot pulsating cock.

Our hips dance in rhythmic motion,
As our bodies gently sway,
Like rippling crests of the ocean,
Surging ecstasy of lust filled waves.

As the dark trembling inside,
Intensifies with your delight,
Like a falling star you now glide,
Towards your orgasmic plight.

Every nerve scatters for cover,
Impulsively you scream my name,
Exalt and decree me your lover,
Torrents gushing upon splayed vein.

You clench upon my glistening member,
Shuddering as the waves now come,
Shouldering my burning ember,
I am your lover,
I am the one.

PJ BAYLISS

LUST'S FIRST TOUCH

I recall my first touch but barely the next,
Life after that is a just black and white mess,
Crisp romance and desire is a climatic blast,
Lust filled longing to caress goddesses clasp.

Toes thrust through the sand as surf spills over feet,
Emotionless shadows resign and copulate in defeat,
Transfixed entanglement with tightening embrace,
Heavenly scented mist of Venus in my face.

The pink surge commences from bosom to torso,
Engorged blood rushes towards her neck also,
Burst of pupil dilation as we gaze eye to eye,
Blurt of your submission seeps across thigh.

Vigorously working resolute solution away,
Silently screaming and beckoning to flay,
Amphitrite's wash breaks loose to soak deep,
Mournful crying of climax as together we peak.

Subdued we release with shuddering spasm,
As I fully explore depths of your sacred chasm,
A glimmer of passion as we silently suspend,
Adorning a look of love I wish will never end.

LUST'S NEXT TOUCH

Our worlds' no longer combine,
Colliding they are separated by time,
I'm left with a postcard of a sun tarnished image,
Of early days when we both looked so fine.

First love sang with a chorus so sweet,
Sandaled in uniform,
Brown hair capturing the breeze,
Her smile transferred to me through a single kiss,
My entire world stood still whenever she appeared.

Years of playful canter and fun,
She was my idol who owned my very soul,
Until that fateful evening she left me,
I was cast forever spinning into love's deepest of holes.

Emerging I clawed away at any light,
Freed at last seemed to have a certain appeal,
Blending into the group,
Bleeding brought under control,
I was quite happy to destroy any new seal.

Society never allowed me to fit,
Top of the wanted list,
Considered as best of friend,
One who could talk,
Be there or be in there,
My induction into lust seemed never to end.

PJ BAYLISS

With lust came romance,
Or so I thought,
Devoid of self conscious I dug myself in so deep,
From bended knee to giving my last ounce of soul away,
Countless cycles before she finally seeped.

My mind parted like a comet in the sky,
Awash of the waters from the beautiful nest,
Now I weep every time I remember,
A lifetime of never ever proving to be her best.

Shut the whole thing down,
Let the mist move in and take total control,
Man the mainsail and drift away,
Barren boy can never swim in that bowl.

I wished for the day we would touch again,
Her silk skin so pure,
Gentle and fine,
My exterior is weathered and worn,
Her absence of touch has neither healed,
Or sealed thee.

Thus my brittle heart is now easily torn,
Exposed once again,
Like my first romance,
Leaves me poised to fall.

To love and to be loved again,
But where the wind takes me,
May not be where I land.

REALIZE

As the glassy glare from lovers face,
Ripped like hunger through my flesh,
I was condemned to depth of forbidden lake,
Forced to rise from my mind's bondage.

Remorsefully I sunk into the pitch-black pool,
In vow of restless silence,
My hunger for passion gnawing away,
With every batch from my appendage.

As chilling echoes of distant love,
Haunted resolute hills and valleys,
Pasture turned to dust underfoot,
As I begged to wade among her seepage.

My outlawed soul surfaced for air,
Absent mind was lost and vanquished,
Upon sight of light from broken pond,
My mind stretched like a bridge.

Lust of sin gushing in torrents,
Rupturing my white skull into half,
Mournfully I shrivel and cry,
Within chilling absence of lovers past.

Her ebb and flow no longer drifts,
Inside me with peaceful harmony or pace,
Forcefully my hand reaches down to key,
To unlatch my mourning hostage.

With a tear creeping from eye I realize.
I would have preferred it if she had killed me.

PJ BAYLISS

INTERNAL FLAME

I feel crowded when I am alone,
Lonely when you enter the room,
This fire burns deep inside of me,
A brand of passion you cannot see.

Waters of lust may dampen the flame,
Quenching my thirst is not my game,
I have opened doors to wade into the deep,
My flame burns bright so long as you seek.

I'm just burning away while they condone,
No matter whom I'm with or if I'm alone,
My flesh is my fare to the sodden earth,
My soul without you simply has no worth.

This is why I dread my daily slumber,
As you charge me with every stupid blunder,
Our vengeance is locked in two pairs of horns,
My patience and love is finally worn.

At night I lay back and emptily stare,
Soaking myself with a wall of tears,
Slowly they seep through my skin,
Damping the fire of passion within.

BIRTH OF MON AMI

I slowly bow down,
You flex with anticipation,
Our lips touch and you sigh from up above,
My lust filled goddess of temptation,
Entomb thy sarcophagus,
Enrapture me.

Silently you release a defining moan,
Compelling me toward,
My head rushes,
Welcoming your king to his throne,
Stream of youth finally gushes,
Catch me.

MY MIST

You do not see it,
Taste, or touch it,
It is simply there,
Like a blank stare.

A void it consumes,
Nothing else resumes,
It permeates and erodes you,
It commands and owns you.

It heeds no other master,
It serves no other.

My Mist,
Feels Bliss.

BLUE TO BLACK

Ripped from my slumber,
Forced to take blue,
So my mind doesn't wander,
And see this night through.

Nothing to explain,
Something on my chest,
Rattling in my skull,
I describe it as best.

Desperately I try,
To avoid taking a white,
It slices me into half,
Confirms my anxious plight.

You have no idea,
How hard I try,
To remain whole,
To enjoy blue skies.

The giggles and laughter,
Echoing within me,
As white takes a hold,
To destroy my anxiety.

I gently shear away,
Gliding through time,
Thoughts disappearing,
Returning in rhyme.

I glide away from this world,
With my Parker beside me,
Not to write,
But to escape with me,
Back,
Into the black.

PJ BAYLISS

DAM

Red to Black,
Tonight it returned,
What left me burnt,
That sharp little edge,
Where sleep is wedged,
Alert tension kicks in,
My precursor to sin.

Swallowing my daily intake,
Four pills make me quake,
Upon my back I rest,
What once was a nest,
Desperate, I try and fall,
Sleep doesn't come at all.

I'm caught between her teeth,
Grit rises from beneath,
Keeps me from sinking,
Silently I'm now thinking…

Dam.

I'm still awake,
Effects of the pill,
No longer a thrill,
Against Doctors order,
More Reds I slaughter,
Double the course,
To remove this remorse.

They ease the pain,
With minor touch of shame,
Still well beneath the dose,
But nothing to boast,
As the numbness kicks in,
Removing any urge to sin.

It's getting so late,
I'm left at the gate,
Effects are finally seen,
Shadows lay where I have been,
A drug induced delay,
Finally,
I'm getting away.

Dam.

I'm splitting,
Sounds now vibrate,
From what's on late
Feet shimmer in zing,
Toes can't feel a thing,
I'm now feeling sliced,
Like a rope,
Un-spliced.

I down another pair,
No longer am I here,
I really wont be missed,
Forever in this abyss.

Dam.

I'm wasted,
Knees weighted with lead,
Motionless as if dead,
I hover above the floor,
Lost and scratching at door.

Room splits into two.
I'm caged in a zoo,
Shadows of beasts now stare,
My mind cannot repair,
Still throwing up a fight,
I chug down a white.

Zing now feels fine,
Washed with white wine,
Now comes the quake,
And my body now makes,
Dashes of blue light,
Crackling across fingers and eyes.

The zing now fills my girth,
Thrown for what I'm worth,
Barely able to lift limb,
Finally sleep begins,
I float down to the floor,
Pinned down like a whore,
Doubling reds and adding white,
Finally takes this world,
From my sight.

Dam,
I'm exhausted.

REALITY BITES

My fate is now done,
After three red and half one,
Blue to see me through,
To ensure I'm absent from you.

It's my own dam plight,
A dream I need to fight,
As running sands of time,
Are flowing throughout my rhymes.

This nightmare only gets worse
And I now edit my verse,
Full crystal glass tilted back
To wash my demons back.

But it's so easy for me
To see what I believe,
My mind splits apart,
Spilling words from my heart.

You fail to understand,
Just how complex I really am,
That I write in order to relieve,
Not just for those that I treat.

Would you prefer a silent bliss?
Or blood pooling from my wrists?
Locked away in my own mind,
Where death itself would be too kind.

Now I'm lost to the blue haze,
Amidst these endless days,
Despite clear skies up above,
Playful giggles and their love.

Try as hard as I may,
I prescribe an end to my day,
This deep slumber at night,
Is now my reality bite.

PJ BAYLISS

RESONATE WITH ME

One night it hit me,
As if a freight train,
Had torn away my voice,
It was in darkness,
When I realized,
I had no obvious choice.

Amidst the darkness,
My life seemed in ruins
Dreams scattered upon the floor,
What once was taken,
Has now become forbidden
Unwelcomed through the door.

My lungs expanded,
A deep sigh captured,
Her scent hanging in the air,
My senses gathered,
What seemed a moment,
Was a lifetime lying there.

Sleep now evades me,
My dreams befriend me,
Through shadows in the dark,
Thoughts are lurking,
Mind is cooking,
Searing it in half.

Slithers of virgin sunlight,
Enter my window,
Embracing me in bliss,
Chasing away the shadows,
Highlighting the subtle,
Scars across my wrists.

Oh, how I remember,
That amber evening,
When I nearly took my life,
As my soul darkened,
When I slowly pealed,
My flesh away with a knife.

The pale yellow fat,
Deep hues of red,
Anointing my plump canvas,
Warm flowing stain,
Releasing my aching pain,
From those who harassed.

Petty words of hatred,
Despise and abuse,
Reinforcing my own fears,
Now these harmless vowels,
Resonate forever,
Between my own ears.

PJ BAYLISS

THE ENEMY WITHIN

I could always feel the cracks,
Long before they appeared,
But to whom could I confide,
Without feeling so weird?

More than a minor headache,
Less than a migraine,
It was just a constant trickle,
A delicate stream of pain.

Resonating with any company,
Echoing whenever alone,
It became my enemy within,
Travelling where I roamed.

It's presence lurked within me,
Chains yanked around the beast,
Conceived from depths of hell,
With a stench like the deceased.

The beast had no master,
That the devil could instruct,
Fists glowing white with tension,
Holding its' chain in my glove.

I released it once or twice,
When preparing to go to war,
The brass rounds were popping,
Blood scattered over the floor.

Seldom few would know,
How my enemy survives,
Or how I restrain its flesh,
Behind my pale hide.

I scoff and laugh if off,
For everyone has their own beast,
Lurking deep within,
Pulling against their leash.

The day my beast escaped,
Cracks snaked across my skull,
A thick grey mist appeared,
Memories became null.

I floated for so many weeks,
Intoxicated while flying,
Mind lost within the clouds,
Sick of people prying.

Now my greatest foe,
The hideous enemy within,
Became my only savior,
As it pulled my bloody head in.

MIND SURGE

This affliction resides in me,
It permeates my noxious dreams,
Forcing me to wake each night,
Compelling me to break and die.

While I reflect upon the past,
Craving each breath was my last,
A last resort is the devil's solution,
Cleansing my mind in ablution.

Poison pumping through my veins,
Ensuring my finest memories fade,
Stripping my loving emotions bare,
Continuously filling my eyes with tears.

No miracles hide within a pill,
Its presence returns when I am blue,
Ripping my tormented skull in two,
A horror that no one else can see,
Nor do they choose to believe.

PJ BAYLISS

My Problem

Somehow, I've managed to survive this situation, so they tell me; "The worst is over..." but do they really know?
Fucking nothing, that's what.

It's my problem.
Not theirs.

I'm the one with nightmares and shadow demons.
I'm the one who hears the echoes of time ticking my head.
It's me that feels the surge of anxiety across my skull.
I experience the electrical side-effects of their medicine.
I've felt the fiery depths of hell burn and fade away within my own eyes.

This barely feels like survival to me.
Co-existence?
Possibly...

I am just another drone that processes each day, every single day. A drone that welds to their wishes and conforms to their expectations. A drone that has to fit into society expectations and normality.

There's no cure for this problem.
This problem is me.
My individuality.
My soul and my inner being.

My fucken remedy!

The old monk must have been right all along...
There does appear to be something golden within me.

To be continued...

Twenty Five

Countless times you've told me,
I am not your cup of tea,
Your opinion does not persuade me,
That you're not the gal' for me.

Countless moments I've gathered,
The pair of us together in my mind,
Forever living life enchanted,
Together throughout space and time.

Forever your words shall haunt me,
Of different stars and a distant time,
Patiently I watch distant galaxies wander,
Forever wishing you will be mine.

When I feel our distance growing,
There is tension within my heart,
My spirit's patience is sorely tested,
For simply missing your infectious laugh.

Words barely describe my feelings,
There's a confession in my soul,
For every moment we are apart,
I realize you once made me whole.

© PJ Bayliss 2025

EPILOGUE (2025)

I reside in rural New Zealand on a property surrounded by native forestry and scenic views of local farmland. It isn't a remote or isolated location; however it is quiet and peaceful with more than enough space between neighbors to be considered secluded and private. It is a lifestyle setting that is picturesque, and for many urban dwellers, considered to be a luxurious part of the country to live in.

It sounds idyllic, doesn't it?

It certainly doesn't sound like a place where one would lose one's mind and fall into the depths of depression and perpetual melancholy. Which is quite ironic given the trigger for my poetry that spilled out of me and fell onto the pages of Burnt.

I wrote Burnt just over a decade ago during a mental hijacking situation trigged by tech burnout. I literally 'greyed out' one afternoon at work while engaged in a large Excel data analysis task that I had to undertake for my employer. The task wasn't anything out of my typical capacity, but it occured after several weeks of repetitive reporting duties and the switch between repetitive task to an analytical processing frame of mind basically tore my brain in half.

To this day I can recall how the screen simply blurred away in front of my eyes. My good friend and team leader must have noticed something was wrong because the next thing I remember was talking to him about if I was fit enough to drive home. Naturally I lied to convince him I could, and my next recollection is that of being on the motorway driving so slowly other motorists were beeping horns as they abused me while they passed by.

I was instructed to see a doctor the following day who initially diagnosed me as being of some party drug or other illicit substance. It was obvious that I couldn't return to work for a while, and I found myself in a prolonged period of unemployment for the following months during my mental health break. It lasted a year in total and we were somewhat fortunate to have some serious savings out aside in the bank for our eventual living expenses.

"Burnt" seemed like such an appropriate title for these poems. They were my personal therapy during my periods of self-isolation in the bedroom, away from everybody I loved. The burned-out sensation in my mind combined with the burning up of our lifetime savings just came to together in an idea to package my emotional confessions and somehow recover a portion of what I had lost.

Admittedly I felt like such a loser for this mistake in my life. The guilt of letting my family down and not being able to contribute plied a heavy weight on my soul. I lied when asked if "I was okay", and my thoughts throughout the day rarely left the realm of self-harm or finding an alternative, unspoken solution to the problem.

The reality is that I was in a high-risk lifestyle situation all along.

The prevalence of depression within rural residents back in that period was not insignificant. Anxiety and depression were higher than the national average, and many people suffering like me refused to seek help by avoiding the topic. Our national suicide rates are 40-60% higher in rural areas than in urban populations. It is a mental health blackspot that continues to be an issue today.

My experience with tech burnout wasn't so commonly reported back in the 2010's, but it obviously crippled me during a prime period of my life. I actually recall having the thread of presence of mind to being aware of the defect in my head within hours of returning home and searching the internet for answers in hope of finding a cure. Somehow offline journalling evolved into writing poetry, and the result is clearly recorded on the pages before you.

The year 2025 has barely commenced as I write this, but it is proving to be one of the most significant years of my life. My decision to release this particular book, along with a couple of my other poetry works, isn't driven by anything other than feeling like I have unfinished business as an author. I started this personal journey over a decade ago as a hobby that provided mindfulness and relief from a busy life.

More recently, I have been guided toward the concept of ikigai by a beautiful soul and a friend that I'm forever in debt to. Our friendship came together somewhat ironically in the very workplace that once destroyed me. Dare I suggest it reminded me that I do have a reason to live, and part of that reason is to write and share my spirit with you, my dearest reader.

Yours forever,
Mon Ami.

www.ingramcontent.com/pod-product-compliance
Lightning Source LLC
Chambersburg PA
CBHW081634040426

42449CB00014B/3314